D1549971

Explaining
Rejection

Steve Hepden

Sovereign World

Scripture quotations are taken from the
NIV The Holy Bible, New International Version.
© Copyright 1973, 1978, New York International Bible Society.
Published by Hodder & Stoughton.

ISBN: 1 85240 077 3

This Sovereign World book is distributed in North America by Renew Books,
a ministry of Gospel Light, Ventura, California, USA. For a free catalog of resources
from Renew Books/Gospel Light, please contact your Christian supplier
or call 1-800-4-GOSPEL.

5 U

SOVEREIGN WORLD LIMITED
P.O. Box 777, Tonbridge, Kent TN11 0ZS, England.

Typeset and printed in the UK by Sussex Litho Ltd, Chichester, West Sussex.

Contents

Acknowledgements

To Chris, without whom it would never have happened,
who in the midst of her own suffering let me go
to fulfil God's purposes;
To my daughters Joanna and Zoe, who have been
so caring and patient with their dad;
The many people who over the years have given themselves
to be counselled by me;
Also my friends in leadership who have trusted and
released me to pray for many hurt and afflicted people.

1

Understanding Rejection

Who would have thought that the 3 year old little girl left at the railway station of the big city was there because her parents didn't want her? The fighting over her revolved around the fact that neither parent wanted her. So finally they both went their separate ways and left her alone at the station.

Ann had become an orphan, yet both her parents were very much alive. She was taken into care and ended up in a famous orphanage where she stayed until her teenage years.

There was nothing hidden about her rejection. It was so open and clear. She wasn't wanted, she wasn't loved, she was thrown away like rubbish. Can you imagine what went on in that little girl's mind? Many say that children are too young to really understand and to be affected. Yet Ann grew up in that orphanage desiring to be loved, to be affirmed, and in her teenage years she reached out for anything possible, no matter what, to satisfy that inner longing for acceptance.

Recently at a wedding where the photographs were taken in a beautiful garden of a house, the old orphanage, Ann showed me the rear fire escape stairs where her boyfriend used to creep in at night, sleep with her then get out quickly before matron did her early morning visits.

Tony had 6 sisters, 5 of them from different fathers, some of them of different colours. Which man was his father? Imagine the confusion, think of the rejection, the pain, the hurt that came through the different men. Insecurity, self-rejection and much more grew out of his childhood and left Tony emotionally crippled. He grew up very sensitive to life, yet this strength became a weakness as he couldn't handle deep relationships.

Years later Ann and Tony became Christians and joined the Fellowship in their home town.

After a very special meeting where the Holy Spirit moved in great power, we prayed for Ann and Tony. They were in different parts of the large ground-floor room of the house. As we prayed for Tony about rejection, Ann reacted severely at the same time as well. The same happened as we prayed for Ann. Tony started to react. This went on for a while. It was amazing to see the Holy Spirit begin to deliver them both at the same time!

Tony and Ann fell in love with each other and got married. They now have a daughter whom they love dearly. There is no rejection. It is gone. They are more secure than ever before. Out of their childhood hurts, wounds and bondages of rejection they have found the love of God and acceptance in each other.

What is rejection?

It is an inability to give or receive love. It is often linked back to childhood, and probably to parents who had the same problem.

Rejection does not mean that there is no love in the home. Often there is some kind of love, but it is what is missing that is important. It may be to do with affection, touch, or the spoken word that builds up or affirms. If they are not there, the symptoms of rejection will be. Rejection is never invited in, it happens, and will affect or ultimately fill the void within us that longs for the security of love.

Someone has said that rejection is the greatest undiagnosed, therefore untreated illness in the Body of Christ today. If that is true and I believe it is, how are we dealing with it and what about people outside of the Body of Christ?

How do people feel rejected?

Sometimes it is not possible to explain it or understand it, only feel it! Many people feel unloved or unwanted and they will soon feel within them a sense of being worthless or valueless. This can lead to inadequacy, inferiority or insecurity. 'Everyone is better than me or does things better than me. I don't feel secure in who I am, I have no identity, no role.' Then guilt enters and you wonder why. Often this leads to self-rejection and you begin a process of speaking negative words to yourself. You have never really liked yourself. Can you change? 'If only I was like him or her…'. This can lead to all sorts of destructive thoughts being entertained.

How can a person who feels rejected handle love or affirmation spoken or shown through affection? All the barriers of self-protection go up, fear of further rejection is around the corner. No one is allowed close.

Rejection affects all relationships

How can a person who feels rejected unconditionally accept the love of God – the Fatherheart of God? It is never easy. Getting close to others is difficult. It is easy to feel rejected by them without much happening. It is easy to put the barriers up and refuse to let others in.

Sometimes people cannot give love because they have not received love or they cannot understand love. You can't receive what you don't recognise. You can't give what you don't possess. So you retreat, and rejection grows a little more.

Rejection can affect every area of a person's life, wounding deeply into the inner personality and spirit. It can happen at any time, although the roots often start in childhood or even in the womb. It may not be recognised in those early years, but rejection is like a seed and will take root as the 'soil' is prepared, and will manifest later. Something like a trauma or negative circumstance can trigger and release it, and another 'layer' of rejection will take place. Remember though, dealing with the fruit will only give temporary relief. The roots need to be recognised, exposed and cut off.

Definition

To refuse to acknowledge or to accept.
To forsake.

To refuse to have or use.
To cast or throw away as useless, unsatisfactory, or worthless.
To discard as not wanted or not fulfilling requirements.
To refuse to love.

Rejection can result from a denial of love. When you are loved you are approved and accepted; when you are rejected you are disapproved and refused.

We all need, require and demand love. God has made us that way. Love develops personal growth, gives a sense of security, develops a healthy and whole life.

Rejection causes a wound of 'self' and problems develop within. The hurt personality will exhibit behavioural patterns and attitudes etc. that are not normal. This will revolve around a crisis of identity and role, which can be a mixture of a withdrawing, protecting, or a rebellious attitude. In my opinion the wound is quite literal and will require healing through prayer and counselling. This may take a while. Probably the emotions too will be affected, and again healing will be necessary. Regretfully we are not immune to the power of the enemy. John 10:10 talks about the devil coming to steal, kill and to destroy, and often people are afflicted by spirits of rejection and possibly others that will be mentioned later. We must not be afraid of this, but realise that Jesus has given us authority in this area to overcome.

The question of so many has been, "Who am I?"; "Where am I going?"; "What am I doing?"; "What is my role?"

Jesus questioned his disciples in Matthew 16:13-16, *"who do people say the Son of Man is?"* Then he said more personally, *"who do you say I am?"* The answer came by revelation. However, the question remains for us too, for if we know who He is, then I believe we can know with certainty who we are!

2

Why Rejection
is a Problem

Mephibosheth was one of the many rejected people mentioned in the Bible. When he was small, some news came that affected him for the rest of his life. His father Jonathan and grandfather Saul were killed in battle (2 Samuel 4:4). Mephibosheth was only 5 at the time and had a nurse who looked after him. She was so shocked and fearful at the news that she suddenly picked him up to run away and hide because she thought Mephibosheth was next. As she was hurrying to leave, he fell, or more likely she dropped him, and he became crippled in his feet for the rest of his life.

Names of characters in the Old Testament are often quite meaningful and give insights into their personalities. Mephibosheth was not only crippled physically at an early age but was certainly crippled inside. The death of father and grandfather caused a great loss. No doubt he felt rejected because they had left him, even in death. He was left with a physical deformity which would isolate him from others and cause a sense of self-rejection, self-hate, inadequacy, inferiority, depression and much more. His name from the Hebrew, it is believed means: *'from the mouth of the shameful thing'*. What positive thing did he have to say? He had lost his rightful inheritance after the death of his family, he grew up a broken man, physically and emotionally and ended up living in the unfortunate place of Lo Debar, which means barrenness, infertile, no pasture.

I know of lots of modern-day Mephibosheths. Affected by the roots of rejection from an early age, crippled within and living in their 'Lo Debars', expressing shame in every area of their lives. Rejection can begin at a very early age and will grow into a major problem. It will become part of them as they mature and develop and in itself will cripple them.

Years later King David who had a good, strong and deep relationship with Jonathan, Mephibosheth's father, asked if there was anyone left in that family that he could help (2 Samuel 9:1-13). The story develops as an old servant of Saul called Ziba mentions Mephibosheth. The King takes steps to help him and puts some proposals to him. His answer is revealing: *"What is your servant that you should notice a dead dog like me?"* He was still full of the past hurts. They hadn't gone away and all he could do was communicate negatively.

Yet the King's word were words of restoration and reconciliation. David gave him back his lost inheritance, and insisted that Mephibosheth eat at his table for the rest of his life as one of the King's sons. It seems that the physical disability was never cured, although it was covered or hidden by the provision of the King's table, and you can be sure that healing within took place.

The heart of our King is to call us to sit at his table. Psalm 23:5 expresses it so well: *'You prepare a table before me in the presence of my enemies. You anoint my head with oil, my cup overflows.'*

We all want the anointing, and we all want our cups to overflow, yet rejection will do its best to stop us sitting at the table to commune with our Lord.

Rejection affects the whole person

The above story indicates the sort of problems rejection can give. It is much more than a small internal thing that affects a person for a short period of time.

More often, it is not the physical that is the root problem. It is within. Simply speaking a person can be divided into 3 areas: body, soul or mind and spirit.

Spirit
When God made man, *'He formed him from the dust of the ground'* and then breathed His life into him, and man became a

living being or soul. Man's spirit was God's gift that brought him life. The human spirit is basically his spiritual source, like the source of a river. Out of this flows his response to life. Someone has said that the spirit is our nature, what we are. It is the aspect of man and woman through which God encounters them, and by which they become aware of and experience Him, a God consciousness. The Bible is very clear that this area of our being can be affected negatively. Proverbs 18:14 explains it clearly: *'a man's spirit sustains him in sickness, but a crushed spirit who can bear?'* Hurts and wounds that come through the circumstances and traumas of life can and will affect our source, our nature, our spirit. Rejection by its definition will affect a person deeply even into their spirit. That is why so many rejected people have problems in their response to God as Father. It seems too that the enemy, in the form of oppression, will affect the spirit and seek to hinder or block any awareness of, and any response to, God.

Soul/Mind

Rejection will also affect the area of the mind or soul. Humans are self-aware and self-conscious beings. The physical body houses the real person, yet is very much joined to it. The personality is formed, simply, by the will, the area of decision, choice or behaviour; the intellect, the area of thought, reason or knowing and the emotions, the area of feeling. Rejection can affect any or all of these areas to the extent that a person is not able to behave as they want, choose as they would like to, or make right decisions. Also, memory can be so affected that these people are able to block out the rejection of the past. Sometimes they are so overwhelmed by past negative situations where the emotions are hidden, that it seems as though they have none. Other times these emotions are so close to the surface, they cannot be controlled. Often all of them intermingle. When you are told that you are no good again and again, it will affect you on the inside. You will behave that way because you believe that you are no good. Your emotions will show others that you believe it; your emotions will show you that it is true, and you will begin to reject yourself.

Body

We need to thank God for our bodies. We also need to be responsible in how we treat them. Some are rejected because they have been told constantly, sometimes for many years, that they are ugly, or made fun of because of certain physical problems. Many people think they are the wrong shape, too big, too small, too thin, too fat, their noses are too long etc. Rejection and self-rejection will not wait to come in, it will afflict you quickly!

Rejection is able to affect any or all of these areas and sometimes deeply. It is also clear that the body, mind and spirit are greatly influenced by each other. You cannot divide them easily. We are not made like that.

Identity and Image

God has called us as individuals with unique personalities. We are all different and we are all important to God. In the beginning God said, *"let us make man in our own image"*. As men and women we image or reflect God's likeness. We are not only made to communicate with Him but also to show Him in the reality of what He represents.

Self-image is the way we see ourselves, a map that we consult about ourselves, what we believe about ourselves. When God made us, He breathed into us His Spirit. This has two faces: God-image and self-image. When we become Christians, the Holy Spirit makes us alive to God. This God-image now in us, works through our self-image to the self-conscious area, i.e. the soul or mind; the will, emotion and intellect. If our self-image is unhealthy, there will be a conflict in the way we see ourselves with the way we know God sees us.

As well as this, our self-image is affected in 3 other areas:-

1. The early years – Parents

As children we totally depend on the reactions around us to arrive at an understanding of who we are. A child is so open and teachable. The most important people in our lives as children were our parents. A child's perception of life is filtered through the words, attitudes and behaviour of its parents. As we look into our childhood mirror, what reflection do we see? We never forget the traumas and negatives of the past years.

2. The world within

Even from childhood we pick up so much of the world's ideas and its rubbish. The way we feel, our senses, our nerves, our capacity to respond, can affect the way we see ourselves, positively or negatively.

3. Satan the accuser

He is the father of lies, the one who will whisper to condemn, to bring guilt, to accuse. He will do what he can to stop us believing that God actually accepts us.

Within us all there is a need for recognition. In Jesus that is fulfilled. Yet it is easy to behave in a certain way to gain acceptance. It is not only children who misbehave to gain attention! Yet in Jesus we not only get peace with God, but with ourselves.

Many of us, however, have learnt over the years to:-
1. Have sculptured faces. We do not reveal the real person.
2. Be conditioned by our environment and people. We have learnt to be what people expect.
3. Act differently depending on who we are with.
4. Hide our true feelings.
5. Construct our image to impress others.
6. Be unreal.

We know that God sent His Son to restore and redeem fallen man and woman and that He was the very stamp of God's nature and being. Yet so often rejection will get to the very root of our identity and image and affect us so deeply, that we cannot live as we want to as Christ's people. We still feel worthless, useless, inferior, inadequate. Proverbs 23:7 says *"as a man thinks, so he is"*. Rejection will make us think and act in a way that is almost the opposite to what we know the Christian life to be. The greatest commandments were summed up very clearly by Jesus:

> *"Love the Lord your God with all your heart, with all your soul and with all your mind and love your neighbour as your self."* (Matthew 22:34-40)

How can you love God and your neighbour if you cannot accept or even love yourself?

Questions:

1. How do you respond when you look in a mirror? Do you feel good?

2. Are you necessary to what God is doing? Do you count? Are you needed? Is there a sense of self-worth and personal value?

3. Are you **really** loved? Do people **really** love you? Is there a healthy sense of belonging? Is there an awareness of being wanted, accepted, cared for, enjoyed and loved?

4. Do you feel that you have the ability to get through life? Do you cope with situations? Are you able to meet life? Do you feel competent?

5. Can you release what you have of God for the Kingdom? Or do you think you are locked up in your self, feeling condemned and guilty?

If we suffer from rejection, we will think that our identity and image is in what we do.

God tells us our identity is in who we are!!

Can demons affect Rejected People?

Rejection violates a person throughout their being. The very character, personality and heart of a person can be affected. Rejection gets to a person's spirit quickly and wounds or bruises it. Rejection will affect the mind or soul of a person causing problems in the area of decision, choice and emotions.

It is clear through experience and counselling that demonic powers can and will come in on the back of these wounds and hurts, which then become a feeding source to them. As the enemy has access to the person via the problem, a bondage will be created. Demons do not respect people and will steal, kill or destroy (John 10:10) as soon as they can, even in the womb or early childhood. Evil spirits will enter into a person's life, or oppress them, because the hurt or wound gives an entrance. The Bible teacher, Derek Prince, says that 'there is a demon behind every negative emotion'. This is the reality of the situation – there is no time for sentiment. We are in a war and the sooner we recognise it the better. Evil spirits cannot enter a person at will. They must have a reason, an open door. Rejection becomes that door and over a period of time with some people, they become demonized.

With others, rejection may be ancestral, generational or inherited. We need to realise that it is quite possible for the children of the parents to be affected by the same wounds and demonic powers linked to rejection. Many times in counselling I have found the source of rejection in a past generation, living or dead. The Bible talks about the sins of the fathers affecting even the third and fourth generations (Exodus 34:6-7).

Hurts wound, bondages bind. So we are left with two areas of healing. One from wounds and one from evil spirits. Mostly it is a mixture of both. We need to learn to discern. We need to trust the Holy Spirit.

Can Christians be affected by demons?

This is a controversial subject in view of the fact that many Christians find being affected by demons confusing. There is no doubt that rejection opens doors for evil spirits to afflict, oppress etc, so a few comments are necessary here. I would draw the reader's attention to another book in this series called 'Explaining Deliverance' which develops this subject.

Consider the following points:

1. Rejection which will leave hurts and wounds within people is a reality.

2. Those hurts and wounds can create a doorway for the enemy to come in to afflict, oppress etc.

3. Evil spirits or demons will attach themselves to that particular wound and will ultimately cause a bondage.

4. Hurts need to be healed, demonic bondages broken.

Question:

If Christians recognise rejection in their lives, is the source just a hurt or is it possible for demonic powers to affect them? I have found backlogs of problems with Christians, partly because these problems have not been recognised over the years. Then suddenly something happens to trigger the rejection and a problem arises. They don't stop being Christians, they deal with the problem! Is it true that when we came into Christianity, we stopped sinning or stopped being sick? No. We are taught to *possess the land* and grow and mature in Jesus and overcome. Yet we sometimes fail. Many Christians have demonic powers affecting them which did not come in after being born again and were there beforehand. The power of the Holy Spirit within and their choice to grow in God has exposed these things.

Comments about demons

1. Demons do not 'possess' people. Although used in some translations, the word possession is not entirely correct.

2. Possession means ownership. Christians have deliberately submitted to the ownership and Lordship of Jesus Christ, not to any demonic power.

3. Demons invade, they do not possess or own! They can and will invade and indwell the mind or soul and body but this is not possession.

4. A better translation is 'to have a spirit'. One of the root words is to be demonized. This denotes a kind of 'fellowship of affliction'. Another word denotes bondage or slavery.

5. So a demon can affect a person in a particular area in their lives, physically, or emotionally and even sometimes in their area of decision making.

6. A demon cannot invade and possess a person's spirit if the Holy Spirit is there. But we have seen that the human spirit can be affected or afflicted by the negative state of the person, emotionally etc, and it seems that through this a demon can hinder or block, but not possess.

7. With regard to rejection, there are certain types of demons that will affect or oppress a person, as well as that person being wounded and hurt by the very act of rejection.

Is Rejection easy to solve?

Basically no! Rejection causes major problems with multitudes of people whether they are Christians or not. It is essential that we do not rush in to solve a problem too quickly, when that person has been hurting for many years. Rejection is a curse on mankind. We need to face it in reality knowing that discernment, patience, mercy, understanding, authority, often discipleship and certainly a greater understanding of the Holy Spirit is required. Without Him we are lost, so get to know Him a little more and trust Him to lead you.

3

The Source of Rejection

In order to appreciate the problems that rejection causes, it is necessary to understand its nature by looking at its beginning. Often people are not aware that their problems are sourced in rejection because they only look at the fruit and do not go further.

The origin of rejection will lead to some surprise. It's source is in the very beginning of humanity, with Adam and Eve and their sons, Cain and Abel. It seems that rejection has been around as long as man and woman.

Bear in mind that the issue here is not roots but source. In order for roots to grow, something has to be planted and the surrounding conditions have to be right. First the ground is prepared, and then the seed is planted. Roots come from that and we will look at those later.

The Garden

This was a place of harmony, of complete relationship where a man and a woman could commune and communicate, that is, have a right relationship with their God. They were fulfilled in their masculinity and femininity, in their sexuality. They were totally affirmed and accepted in their identity, and quite secure in their role. There was a true sense of worth and belonging as they lived in the garden and met with God. Genesis 1:31 sums it up: *'God saw all that he made and it was very good'*. Not good, but very good! Often Adam and Eve heard *'the sound of God'* walking in the garden and they were at one with Him.

It was here where God gave the man and woman a commission which was to last for ever. In Genesis 1:28 *'God blessed them and* said to them, *"Be fruitful and increase in number; fill the earth and subdue it. Rule over every living creature"'*. So in the beginning God said, *"be fruitful"*, which is sexuality; *"subdue"*, which is authority and *"rule"*, which is spirituality. This was to be man and woman in their truest calling and capacity. God gave them everything they required to live on this earth with satisfaction and fulfilment.

The Enemy

It was in this fantastic location, where the man and woman were so satisfied, that Satan came to tempt them. True fulfilment only comes with choice and God had not only commissioned them, but gave them some commands that they were to obey. Satan hit at the heart of the issue when he undermined Adam and Eve's relationship with God and with each other. He tempted them with what he called *'so much more'*. He challenged them in their role and identity. "Why, your eyes are not yet opened, there is so much more to see and to know, you will be like God", he said. He deceived them with 'you will be and you will know'.

Nothing changes over the years, does it! He undermined God's Word, gave them false expectations, distorted their image of themselves as children of God, and then destroyed their relationship with God and damaged their relationship with each other.

The Choice

God gave the man and woman free will, a right to choose, therefore they had responsibility. They decided to reach out for more, far beyond where they were. There was nothing more of course, except deception, and they lost far more than they realised. God has given us all a right to decide about issues. We have the ability to make right or wrong choices. Adam and Eve made a wrong choice and we have all suffered for it. They not only disobeyed God but rebelled against Him and therefore rejected Him. They chose rejection and the damage was done. Their eyes were certainly open and instead of innocence there was shame.

The Curse

Usually when God came into the garden, there was joy and great fellowship. This time Adam and Eve were hidden, they were afraid, they had rejected God's ways. God asked why, and neither the man or woman would take responsibility. The man blamed the woman and the woman blamed the Devil (Genesis 3:11-13). God made them all accountable. They had lost their spiritual, mental, emotional and physical harmony with each other and God. Because they rejected Him, He rejected them from the garden and that disobedience became a curse to them as they went into a fallen world. They lost their spirituality, their authority, and their inheritance, and death had set in. They could not go back. Their role and identity were undermined and in my opinion great disappointment came on them as they left the garden. You can be sure that the enemy took great advantage by putting many negatives on Adam and Eve, including rejection. Regretfully the consequences were soon to affect their first two sons, and rejection quickly became a root.

The Sons – Cain and Abel

Adam and Eve were isolated, lonely and damaged. Their rejection of God and of His Word had turned in on them. They felt, and were, a rejected couple. Even the animals and the land seemed against them.

It was into this that the boys were born. Cain was the first and Abel came next (Genesis 4:1-2). How different they were. This difference was manifest in their response to God which is clearly summed up right at the end of the New Testament in 1 John 2:12. *'Do not be like Cain, who belonged to the evil one and murdered his brother. And why did he murder him? Because his own actions were evil and his brother's were righteous'*. That is an amazing statement. Why was there such a difference? Cain was not given over to Satan, but somehow Satan had a clear effect on him.

Cain was the firstborn and it seems that something of the rejection of the parents had passed into him. There is something about the firstborn that is important. Throughout Scripture the firstborn has significance. Abel offered the firstborn of his flock to God (Genesis 4:4); firstfruits of the harvest were a special offering to God (Deuternomy 26:1-4); God said to Moses to go to Pharaoh and say *"Israel is my firstborn son, let my son go"*. Maybe Satan was aware of the special nature of the firstborn and wanted to destroy it right at the beginning.

There was also another reason. There was a generational link of the sins of the parents. Something had come through and clearly affected Cain, and his sense of choice, reason, and behaviour showed it. He was more affected than his brother. Adam and Eve had given Satan a right and that did not finish with them. The whole of the human race had been affected. Some would say that is not fair. I agree, life is not fair, yet even in Cain's sin and disobedience, God gave him another chance, as we shall see.

The Offerings

Abel kept flocks and Cain worked the soil (Genesis 4:2-5). Cain brought the fruits of the soil as an offering to God, and Abel brought the fat portions of the firstfruits of his flocks to Him. God accepted Abel's, but not Cain's. Why?

First of all realise that God had just cursed the ground (Genesis 3:17), and the serpent (Genesis 3:14), but not the rest of the animal life. How could you bring an offering to God from that which He had just cursed?

Secondly, look at Cain's motive and attitude. Cain wanted to please God by what **he** had done. He wanted God to accept the works of **his** hands and affirm **him** for what **he** had done. Selfish? Yes. Not only that, but Cain was worshipping the works of his own hands rather than worshipping God, which is idolatry. Look at Hebrews 11:4 *'by faith Abel offered God a better sacrifice than Cain did. By faith he was commended as a righteous man, when God spoke well of his offerings. And by faith he still speaks, even though he is dead'*. Abel offered by faith, Cain offered by works. Cain offered because he wanted acceptance and affirmation for selfish reasons, Abel offered as a response to God and God alone.

The Reaction

The Bible says that Cain was not just angry but **very** angry, and his face was downcast, or sad. There was a mixture of depression and self-pity, and he began to be rebellious. God had looked with favour on Abel's offering but he did not receive Cain's at all. What an incredible reaction Cain had. Who was he angry with? God, or Abel, or both? It was as though Cain was acting like a spoilt little boy who was unable to get his own way.

Yet look at God's response. Genesis 4:6 says that God came back to Cain to enquire why he was upset. Can you see grace and compassion here? *"Why?"*, asks God and then comes the key, in Genesis 4:7, *"if you do what is right, will you not be accepted?"* God begins to reason with Cain and gives him an opportunity to get it right. Yet Cain wanted it right **his** way, not God's way. If God appeared to you and said "do it my way not your own", would you change in order to get it right? So would I! The issue revolves around the word 'if'. Obedience will mean acceptance, disobedience will mean rejection.

The Warning

This is the critical stage. God gives a warning to Cain in Genesis 4:7, *"if you do not do what is right, sin is crouching at the door; it desires to have you, but you must master it."* God in His grace prophesies to Cain. He is telling him what is happening in the spiritual realm. He is saying that there is still a chance to get it right. He is showing Cain that the enemy is waiting at his door. The root word for 'crouch' or 'lies' (Authorised Version) is linked to a demon waiting at the door of a building to threaten the people inside. Therefore God is warning Cain of the seriousness of the situation he is in, and of the choice he has to make. God also made clear Cain's personal responsibility in this matter. It is never just the demonic, or even personal hurts. Personal responsibility is vital. It seemed that Cain wanted to blame everyone else rather than take some responsibility himself. The word master means to overcome. Would God say that kind of thing if He didn't mean it? If He says we can overcome, by His grace and in His name, we can!

The Judgement

Cain took no notice but deceived Abel by enticing him into a field where he killed him (Genesis 4:8). The hatred and anger was somehow released onto his own brother. Of course God knew what had happened but asked the question in order to get a response from Cain. He replied in a defiant manner with a lie and then followed that up with the totally rebellious comment, *"am I my brother's keeper?"* He was hard, insensitive, and indifferent.

The result was a curse. Cain had every opportunity to change and be accepted. He took none of it and basically God's hands were tied. Cain became his own victim. He had rejected God and His ways and became rejected by God. He became a marked man and was commissioned to be a restless wanderer throughout the earth.

These words are such a key in rejection. Rejection is tied up with identity and image. The restless wanderer never finds fulfilment in who he or she is. There is no satisfaction in his role as a person. Something is always driving him 'to something more'. Unfortunately like Adam and Eve, and now Cain, 'something more' is never there. This restlessness is a control which drives a person so that they are never satisfied in who they are, and what they do. This is the source of rejection. Cain reacts further (Genesis 4:13-14), saying to God, *"my punishment is more than I can bear"*. This is self pity and probably self rejection. *"You are driving me from the land"*; *"I will be hidden from your presence"*. This is Cain putting the blame and responsibility on God. *"Whoever finds me will kill me"*. This is fear of rejection and fear of death.

Summary

1. We need to be aware of the significance of these early passages in Genesis and their link to rejection, for the source and roots of rejection are manifest there.

2. It is clear that rejection has been around as long as man and woman have been living, The lives of the first family are such a key to rejection. We need to take note.

3. Rejection can be hereditary as well as affecting us in our daily lives.

4. Satan and his demonic powers have a great part to play in rejection.

5. Our power to choose, our free will, what we want, also has an important part in rejection. We have a personal responsibility, and we need to understand this.

We have a command from the Scripture; *'do not be like Cain'* (1 John 3:12-15) and from the book of Jude, who judges those who have *'taken the way of Cain'* (Jude 11).

We need to consider this seriously because it would appear rejection has affected many, if not all of us, in some way or other.

4

The Roots of Rejection

What are Roots?

When seed has been planted and the conditions are right, it is not long before roots begin to grow. Roots are the hidden parts, yet so vital to the whole. The roots of a tree anchor and give support to it. They are its source of feeding and nourishment. Long and deep they become in length under the ground, often as tall as the tree itself. Anyone who has been involved in exposing and digging out roots of any plant, shrub, tree or weed, will understand how difficult and lengthy a job it is.

We cannot ignore the roots of rejection. They are often deep, strong, have developed for many years, and therefore will need careful and sensitive handling when they become exposed, ready to be cut off.

It is easy to pick the fruit from a tree. It is fairly straightforward to deal with fruit in a person's life. However, if the roots are not dealt with, the fruit will return time and time again and cause frustration. In Amos 2:9 it says, *'I destroyed his fruit above and his roots below'*. In view of the nature of rejection, and the fact that often it affects people for many years, understanding and identifying its roots becomes vital.

The Roots of Rejection

There are three areas which seem to sum up the roots of rejection. Later we will look at the fruit and causes of rejection, and although they are many and varied, it seems clear that they come out of only three roots, listed below:

1. Rebellion or Rebelliousness

In the context of rejection, rebellion is seen as an aggressive reaction, which shows itself in opposition, or defiance, to the person who is perceived to show rejection. When the rejected person reacts in this manner, anyone who gets in their way can be affected. The emotional reaction can be expressed through a display of possibly anger, arrogance or criticism which can remain deeply hidden. At some stage, there will probably be an eruption like a volcano and damage may be done to them and to anyone around them. Many people with this root just hurt themselves. This can be through hating themselves, cursing themselves with a negative word, or being physically violent to their own bodies, causing destruction.

There is a definite link with rebellion and witchcraft. Samuel said to Saul, *"for rebellion is like the sin of divination or witchcraft, and stubbornness or arrogance is like iniquity and idolatry. Because you have rejected the word of the Lord, he has rejected you as king"* (1 Samuel 15:23). Remember Cain? Often spirits of witchcraft are behind rebellion and control (see later) and the problem becomes much greater.

2. Self-Rejection

This is a reaction whereby the person who is rejected turns that rejection into themselves. They take on the rejection in such a way that they begin to reject themselves. It becomes amazingly negative and totally self-orientated. It can lead to the road of destruction called suicide. That may be a long way ahead but roots are strong and powerful and will not stop growing while being fed by thoughts, words and actions of self rejection. It is not difficult to turn thoughts of rejection inward. Yet when we reject ourselves, we will finally reject the God who made us.

3. Self-Protection

This is also known as **fear of rejection**. Fear is always around the corner when rejection affects a person. The fear of additional hurt will create or release defence barriers that prove difficult to get through. Can you trust anyone? Will you be hurt again by that same person? You put up a barrier to protect yourself. You close off those inner feelings or emotions. You take control and no-one is going to get close enough to damage you again. Sometimes people in this state become emotionless, by getting to the stage where they won't allow themselves to be emotional anymore.

Points to Note

1. An interesting fact is that these roots appear differently. How can they all link to rejection? Basically rejection does not just affect one type of person. It affects any person, of any character and personality. This means that there will be different ways people react, therefore rejection could manifest in any or all of the three roots. It is quite common for some to be affected by all three. The memory, the will and the emotions can be influenced differently, which causes attitude and behaviour change.

I have counselled people who react in both ways and manifest all three roots. For example, a man feeling unable to get through to God because he could not respond to Him as father and whose emotions were so locked up, was found to have been rejected in early childhood. That left a strong reaction of anger and hate (rebellion), a deep insecurity, inadequacy and inferiority (self-rejection), and fear of failure, of being dominated, criticism and pride (self-protection). That man expressed anger and hate (outward reaction), and the deep hurts had blocked off early memories so that he could not weep (inward reaction).

2. It is clear that these roots can be demonic in their own right. There are demons called rebellion, self-rejection and self-protection. We need to **learn to discern** whether they are demons, or wounds, or both. Besides these root areas, there is a demon called rejection in its own right. The three roots in themselves point clearly to rejection. Just as the trunk of a tree grows out from its roots, so rejection is recognised by its roots, and often a demon is behind it.

3. Another demonic power to be considered is the 'Orphan Spirit'. This is often clearly linked with rejection, and roots in the very early months or years of a person. We are made with a need for love, care, affection, touch, cuddles and right discipline. We require that kind of love, it brings us security. Many people as children do not receive any kind of love from their parents and this causes a wound, and ultimately a spirit will seek to oppress that person. It is as though they are orphaned because they are deprived of the love of one or both parents. Anger and resentment even at an early age will begin to affect them, as well as the roots of rejection. People affected by this spirit find it hard to respond to the Fatherheart of God. How can they when they do not receive love from their earthly fathers?

4. Control is also vital to be considered in the area of rejection and it can be linked to any of the roots. Control is a conscious or unconscious power over another person. It can be manifest as domination, superiority or emotional manipulation. It has everything to do with rejection, because in order to feed the problem, circumstances, situations or people have to be controlled.

Control also happens as people suppress emotions, memories or hurts of rejection. They create a defence and will not allow themselves to be hurt again and often they will not release any emotions. The dam that is created is a hard and harsh reaction covering up so much hurt. Ultimately a spirit of control may come in behind the dam and a bondage will be created. Many people I know have come into Christianity with this control, and they soon find they cannot release their emotions, worship as they wish, or be open to the moving of the Holy Spirit. They will need release. It is vital to discern these roots.

There is another area of control, which is much more outward. It is domination which comes out of rejection. Rejected people have a fear of domination or fear of further rejection and they will, if given the right, control in order to make sure they don't get hurt. They may do this through a form of conditional love. In other words, the person is controlled by the threat of withdrawing that love. This can happen in childhood. The person who is rejected can easily become dependent on the rejected one, and use that as a form of control. Control can lead to the 'Jezebel' spirit (Revelation 2:20-23) affecting a person. This spirit will dominate, accuse or transfer guilt, release anger, deny responsibility or cause infirmity, and it has links with religiousness and sexual perversity.

Also it is necessary to look at the reaction of the 'little boy' or 'little girl'. Again this is more apparent than one realises. These reactions happen in a number of ways. Often with rejection in the early years the hurt child goes within itself because it cannot cope, or is not allowed to cope with the trauma. The child becomes locked up and it is often years later before the emotions come out. I have met many adults who are in part still little boys or little girls. They react very emotionally in situations they cannot handle. They are aggressive, dominant, manipulative, withdrawn, insecure and much more. The problem grows when a demonic bondage enters in. I believe there are demons called 'the spirit of the little boy' or 'the spirit of the little girl'. Of course the emotions need releasing and healing, yet often demonic powers are there as well. It has been important to be sensitive when dealing with people affected in this way because no adult likes being called a hurt little girl or little boy.

Control has a close link with another demonic power, called witchcraft. The Holy Spirit will be grieved by situations of wrongful control, because its character is domination and manipulation. Spirits of witchcraft will come into the vacant area. It is a strong occult spirit and the control, which feeds the rejection, will soon open the door to these spirits. It is not hard to exercise control over someone, and if rejection is driving you it becomes all the easier.

5

The Fruit of Rejection

What is Fruit?

Fruit can be defined as the product or result of something. As a seed is sown, it will root into the ground and ultimately produce – usually above ground – a fruit, consisting of a body with a seed in it. Sometimes it is edible.

Rejection produces fruit. It is important to understand and recognise the fruit of rejection in view of the importance of distinguishing roots. It is also easy to identify the fruit, and deal with it, without touching the root. Often this happens, and a problem develops when the fruit returns. It is essential then to cut the root as well as pick the fruit.

Reactions

A reaction is a particular response to a situation.

With rejection, reaction comes in two forms. It is important to understand these areas because the roots of rejection which are affecting people will manifest in either or both of these ways.

First: outwardly, visible or external

Here people can be over-emotional, expressing all kinds of outward and loud emotions such as anger, be overbearing in behaviour, or aggressive in attitude. Rejected people sometimes defend themselves by attacking others. They are fearful of any more rejection so they put up defensive barriers, while at the same time reacting against someone else.

Secondly: hidden or internal

Here there may be a controlled suppression of the emotions, which can be like a dam. Things can be hidden which go back years but still have an effect. Rejected people often escape into themselves. They don't seem to cope with reality. It seems easier to hide, and not communicate honestly.

In both areas the response is unconscious. In other words people do not know why they react as they do, and often they fail to cope with everyday life. So the real person is not seen. This will affect identity and role, which in turn will affect the whole of their lives.

Words

The way the fruit of rejection is recognised is usually through words. Words explain, reveal and inform. I want to introduce you to the three lists of words which describe the three roots of rejection. The meaning of these words will give you an understanding as to the identification of these roots in your life. The more we relate and respond to these words in our own character and personalities, the more a picture is built up, which gives an indication of the root of rejection. For example, look at the word insecurity, which means a lacking in confidence in situations, or to be unsure or unstable. If that is a weakness in character, it may, alongside other key words highlight the possibility of a root of self rejection. Obviously this is not so in isolation, but linked with a response to other words listed; so a picture begins to build up.

In Counselling

I often use these words as a type of test or study as I begin to counsel people whom I sense have a root of rejection. I go through every word quite quickly, asking them to apply the various words to their own lives, and encouraging them to look honestly at their character and personality to identify any weaknesses related to those words.

In order to assist them, I ask them to mark themselves on a scale of 1 to 5; 5 being 'yes, this word really relates to me', down to 1 being 'No, this word is not me'. It is important to discern how far back you go over the years. Sometimes it is necessary to go as far as the memory allows.

As the marks are added in the word groupings, anything over 50% of one section is an indication of that specific root. Often it can be important to involve someone close to the person or the other half of the marriage, in order to get their opinion and confirmation. It is vital to be honest.

Let's look at the 3 groupings of words which make up the fruit of rejection (there are obviously more). As we look at them and maybe use them in our process of discerning roots, be sensitive to the Holy Spirit pinpointing any weaknesses.

Realise too that some of these fruits may be demonic in their own right, or they may be the reaction of the flesh which will feed the roots of rejection. We must learn to discern and to trust the Holy Spirit to direct us. If these areas are demonic, they can be dealt with accordingly, but remember discipleship will always be necessary whether demonic or fleshly.

Each word is given a definition to help understand the meaning.

Fruit relating to Rebellion or Rebelliousness

Harshness: Being severe, rough, usually verbally.

Rejection of others: This can happen when rejected people come under pressure in relationships.

Hardness: Strong, not easily penetrated, unyielding.

Unbelief: Refusal or inability to believe, for, or in self.

Scepticism: A strong or undermining attitude or doubt.

Defiance: Hostile, resistant, openly disobedient.

Criticism: Finding fault or imperfections.

Arrogance:	A feeling of superiority shown in an overbearing manner.
Stubbornness:	Will not give way, unyielding.
Anger:	Varied emotional reactions linked to loss of control.
Violence:	Either to self or others, words or actions.
Bitterness:	Full of resentment.
Drugs:	Any kind of medical substance or stimulant that may remove emotional pain.
Occult:	Any involvement is disobedience to God.
Legalism:	An over emphasis of principle in any situation, i.e. home or church.
Lust:	Strong or excessive desire, i.e. power, sex, recognition, ambition, materialism.
Control:	With self, i.e. emotions or dominating others.
Aggression:	Offensive, hostile.
Refusal of affection:	Will not accept comfort after a rejection situation.
Argumentative:	Given to quarrels and disputes.
Revenge:	To retaliate, to pay back with word or deed.

Fruit relating to Self-Rejection

Low self-image:	"I am of no value."
Inferiority:	"Everyone does it better than me."
Inadequacy:	"I can't."
Sadness:	An unhappy feeling, sometimes intense, mournful.

Sorrow:	An anguish, heartache due to loss.
Grief:	Deep or violent sorrow, great distress.
Shame:	A painful emotion related to one's own behaviour, disgrace, humiliation.
Guilt:	A feeling of doing something wrong.
Self-accusation:	"I am guilty, wrong." Putting self down.
Self-condemnation:	"I need to be punished." Cannot accept commendation.
Inability to communicate:	Something deep hindering communication, which may be stubbornness, or sulking.
Fear of failure:	"I can't cope with it happening again." Panic attack.
Insecurity:	Uncertain, unconfident.
Disappointment:	Failure to fulfil desires or expectations.
Loneliness:	"I have no one." Isolation.
Hopelessness:	"It's gone too far, there is no way out."
Wrong expectations:	Assuming too much, or getting into wrong situations.
Seeking to please:	A pressure to please from a wrong motive.
Anxiety:	Troubled, uneasy, fretful.
Worry:	Dispirited, dejected, low, heavy.
Infirmity:	Self-rejection can bring physical problems.

Fruit relating to Self-Protection

Pressure to perform:	"I must be effective in order to gain acceptance."

Striving:	Trying too hard, conflict, strenuous effort.
Restlessness:	An internal driving, giving no rest.
Pressure to achieve:	"I must be successful in order to gain acceptance."
Competitiveness:	"I must be superior in all I do."
Independence:	"I can do without you, I can do it on my own."
Self-centredness:	"It's only me I'm interested in."
Self-justification:	Always seeking to excuse yourself.
Self-righteousness:	Always right, never wrong in own eyes.
Criticism of others:	Finding fault, disapproving, undermining.
Judgementalism:	A hurtful, hostile, injurious, authoritative pronouncement, often to or about someone.
Jealousy:	Suspicious of another who is receiving what you want.
Envy:	A deep, strong desire to have what another has.
Self-pity:	A feeling of sadness and sorrow for self.
Pride:	A high opinion of one's own qualities.
Possessiveness:	A strong desire to hold onto something or someone, linked to control.
Perfectionism:	"I must get it right." Faultless.
False gratification:	Finding satisfaction or comfort, which only distracts from rejection, e.g. food, sex, nicotine, drink, drugs (illegal or prescribed).

Self-deception:	"I can't hear God." "No one understands me."
Fear of betrayal:	"How can I trust anyone anymore?"
Unreality:	Withdrawal into a shell. Avoidance of the problem.
False responsibility:	Covering up rejection by working for God. "To get recognition, I will do anything for God."
Shyness:	Uneasy in company or avoiding company, timid.

6

The Many Causes of Rejection

Causes

A cause is a reason or action that makes something happen.

It is important to see that there are many causes that bring rejection and that it is possible to be affected, at the beginning of life, or at any time throughout it. We need to look into these specific areas because it is from these that the roots and fruit of rejection develop.

Conception

Rejection can begin in the form of a wound, hurt or demonic oppression before a child is born. The enemy is no respecter of persons. It is a fact that many adults have found that the roots of their problems have been sourced in childhood or even earlier.

Consider this reference from 'The Secret Life of the Unborn Child' by Verney and Kelly, Sphere Books 1981.

Quote: "We now know that the unborn child is an aware, reacting human being who from the sixth month on (and perhaps earlier) leads an active emotional life. Along with this startling find we have made these discoveries:

a)   The foetus can see, hear, experience, taste and, at a primitive level, even learn **in utero** (that is in the uterus – before birth). Most importantly, he can FEEL – not with an adult's sophistication, but feel nonetheless.

b)   A corollary to this discovery is that what a child feels and perceives, begins shaping his attitudes and expectations about himself. Whether he ultimately sees himself (and hence acts), as a happy or sad, aggressive or meek, secure or anxiety-ridden person depends, in part, on the messages he gets about himself in the womb!"

Therefore it is clear that a denial of love can affect a child before it is born. The womb becomes the child's first home. Is it friendly or unfriendly, peaceful or hostile? The child will receive both parents' feelings and thoughts. Their attitude and relationship with the child before it is born will affect it after it is born.

The following are reasons for rejection before birth:-

● An unwanted pregnancy.

● Illegitimacy. Look at Deuteronomy 23:2 which talks about a curse of 10 generations. This can be cut off in Jesus' name. It is possible for conception outside of marriage to produce a demonic oppression of poverty, uncleanness and insecurity.

● Already has too large a family.

● Financial problems.

● Conception too soon after marriage.

● Fear of the birth, fear of deformity.

● Attempted abortion.

● Babies born to women who have become pregnant through rape, incest, adultery, or mothers who were alcoholics or dependent on drugs.

● Separation or divorce before the baby is born. More often than not the child will take the blame.

● A shock or trauma during pregnancy such as an accident or the death of someone close, family or friend.

● The mother becoming pregnant at quite a late age, i.e. over 40.

It doesn't matter what the reasons are, the enemy is no

respecter of persons and he will be wanting to get in to wound or oppress.

It is good to know, however, that God is very concerned about children in the womb and Scripture is so encouraging and comforting.

The Psalmist puts the word of the Lord so clearly in Psalm 139:13-17:

> *'It was you who created my inmost self, and put me together in my mother's womb; for all these mysteries I thank you: for the wonder of myself, for the wonder of your works.*
>
> *You know me through and through, from having watched my bones take shape when I was being formed in secret, knitted together in my mother's womb.*
>
> *You had scrutinized every action, all were recorded in your book, my days listed and determined, even before the first of them occurred.'*

The Birth

It is clear that rejection can be caused by the actual birth or soon afterwards.

● The pain, pressure, isolation and loneliness of a long birth can put the mother and even the father under great mental pressure. Sometimes things can be said that are later regretted.

● The opposite can also affect the child, such as the shock of a fast delivery or a caesarean birth or a birth with instruments.

● Some babies need special attention or surgery at birth. An emergency may take it away from its mother. Suddenly the baby is out of its 9-month secure home and without any bonding is taken away and put in a strange box (incubator) with all sorts of wires attached to it.

● The mother's death at the birth of her baby.

- After being born, the baby may immediately be taken away and adopted.

- Feeding problems caused by fear, insecurity or medical problems.

- If the mother or father or both have known rejection, it is probable that rejection will manifest in the baby. How parents show love, acceptance and affection is important.

- Sex preference can be a serious issue for some parents. If both or one of the parents show disappointment in the sex of their child, it is possible that problems may show up in the future. 'We wanted a boy and you are a girl' or 'we wanted a girl and you are a boy'. Whose fault is it? Often the children take the guilt on and feel rejected. Sometimes the problem grows if the couple felt 'the Lord' had shown them. Who gets the blame? The child will ultimately come to hate and reject itself and may perform as the opposite to gain attention. Sometimes other spirits gain access such as lesbianism or homosexuality.

- Not calling the child a name for a long time (I know of a child that was not named for 6 months!).

- Being a "replacement child", conceived because the other one died!

- Parents or doctors not realising that there was a second baby in the womb!

Infancy

Rejection will also affect a child as it is growing up. It can be seen that the first few months and years of a child's life are foundational and formative. Children mirror those that are close to them, parents, family etc, and their spirits are wide open to influence. They will take things on whether positive or negative.

- Words affect children, i.e. 'you were a mistake', 'we didn't want any children', 'we didn't want you, we wanted a boy', 'we didn't want you, we wanted a girl', 'I wish you had never been born'. Life and death is in the power of the tongue (Proverbs 18:21).

- Sometimes children are separated too long, too early in life from their parents. However legitimate this separation is, we need to be careful.

- Children given up for adoption in their early months or years.

- Preferential treatment of one child over others can cause rejection. It may cause attention seeking and friction between the other children.

- The trauma or shock of death, divorce or separation. It is seen as a great loss to the child.

- Physical disabilities or speech impediments which affect a child's learning ability.

- Prolonged childhood illness or hospitalisation can bring isolation.

- The way parents talk, confront, argue in front of their children can bring insecurity and ultimately rejection. Children blame themselves easily.

School Life and Teenage Years

Rejection can start or continue into the very important years up to adulthood. There are many changes and decisions to face and therefore how we see ourselves can affect what we turn out to be.

- Children who are over-criticised, over-disciplined, dominated, ignored or favoured over the others will be open to rejection.

- Being sent to boarding school.

- Being bullied, unfairly treated by teachers or children.

- Embarrassing incidents at school leading to self-rejection.

- Parents can put their children under pressure to succeed which will lead to guilt, perfectionism and self-rejection.

- Disinterest of parents to school work.

- Religious pressure on children from parents can cause legalism, traditionalism and inflexibility which will lead to self-rejection.

- Personal comments such as, "I'm no good"; "I'll never make it"; "I'm too fat, too thin, too tall, too short, my nose is too big/long"; "I want to be someone else". These comments need to be taken seriously if made.

- Exclusion from group of friends, being called names.

- Being laughed at in class, not understanding what is being taught.

- Being put down in school or home, not allowed to have an opinion.

- Constant sickness causing academic problems will affect self-worth.

- Injustice in being punished wrongly.

- A teacher always picking on a student, ridiculing them.

- Pressure from parents because brother or sister has done better.

- The start of long term chronic illness in teenage years will cause problems of rejection.

- Guilt over a teenage pregnancy, sexual experience or abortion.

Family Rejection

What goes on within the family and between the family is so important in the development of relationships between parents and children. There is so much that can cause the roots of rejection. Many people have suffered in this way.

- Being called names by family members emphasising personal features.

- Constant criticism in the family.

- Poverty in the family.

- Immigration difficulties, i.e. language, racism. Often children are in the forefront of the problem of translation etc.

- Speech or learning difficulty, i.e. stuttering, dyslexia.

- Domination by one member of the family.

- Cruel parents.

- Unhappy parents.

- Alcohol or any other addiction in the family.

- Embarrassment over religious beliefs.

- A family member convicted of a crime.

- Parents showing no interest or active interest in the development of the child.

- Being an only child, possibly spoilt, possessed, dominated.

- Lack of affection in the family, i.e. "we don't talk about things like love"; "we are not a demonstrative family"; "we get embarrassed".

- Redundancy or long periods of unemployment.

- Financial disasters.

- Separation, broken engagement, divorce.

- Sexual abuse whether inside or outside the family.

- A women or a man feeling that they are not physically attractive.

- Being ashamed of one's sex.

- An inability to communicate by either or both parents. It is vital to talk, to show by action that you care and love one another.

- Being forced into adult responsibilities in childhood or teenage years.

- Ill treatment by step-parents.

- Being forced by parents into wrong behaviour, i.e. stealing, immorality.

- The premature death of parents or any other member of the family.

- Being an only child and over-protected.

- Being a middle or youngest child and ignored.

- Being the eldest child with unrealistic expectations put on you.

- Coping with the fact that you have been adopted and you don't know your real parents.

- Being a handicapped or disabled person.

- Children that are fostered express rejection.

- Children rejecting their parents especially when they are old.

- A refusal to have sexual relations in marriage.

- Unfaithfulness in the marriage.

- An inability to have children.

- Being evacuated in time of war.

All of these areas are important and need to be considered sensitively. However I wish to comment further on two of them.

Abuse

This is becoming more and more common and often begins in the early years of life. There are different types of abuse which need to be considered. It is clear too that these types of abuse happen in marriage.

1. Verbal or mental abuse is any form of negative pressure by thoughts or words. Adults as well as children can be "put down" easily by words or the mental pressure of long silences or talking to others and ignoring you. Injury comes easily, particularly in childhood, and the results lead to hurt, locked up and demonised people. Remember the power of the tongue!

2. Physical abuse is everywhere today through childhood and into marriage. Although the physical side is horrible, consider the emotional hurt and humiliation which a person suffers and the length of time it may take to heal. There is a right way to discipline a child!

3. Sexual abuse is also very common today inside and outside marriage. It creates deep wounding and much demonic activity including rejection and particularly self-rejection. Most abuse is suppressed and buried deep within a person, and more often than not the reason is that the problem lies within the family. If a child or young person is abused from within their family, the guilt, fear and confusion will be great, and they will endure the shame because of loyalty or the fear of reprisals or threats. There will be negative results in later life whether the person gets married or not. There is always a violation of dignity, sexuality and humanity which will bring its own problems, especially in marital relationships. The person will grow up with a sense of defilement and will be in conflict, with hate, fear and distrust.

Abuse means betrayal. This leads to rejection.

Rejection in Marriage

Separation and/or divorce will lead to some form of rejection. Whoever is right or wrong in the situation isn't ultimately the problem. It is the reaction and attitude of both parties to the other and the way they feel about themselves. The confession before God, one another and witnesses creates a spiritual bond. It is often declared in Church, "whom God has joined, let no man divide or put asunder". The tearing that separation and divorce brings causes deep wounding and often deep rejection. This can be so difficult for Christians and even those in leadership. We need to be aware of the sense of being cast aside, the worthlessness, the pain and rejection felt, notwithstanding losing income, home, friends and schools, often with children losing relationship with one or both parents.

Summary

We need to see that rejection can affect most if not every area of our lives. This is why it is so important that we understand its significance in the foundations of our lives and of its impact spiritually so that we can face up to it in the power of the Holy Spirit.

7

Jesus and Rejection

The key to all we have been looking at with regard to rejection lies in Jesus. There was no one more rejected that Jesus. Someone has said that he was the most rejected person who ever lived. If this statement is true, it says that Jesus must have identified with rejection in his life and death in a way that cannot be compared with anyone else.

We have seen that rejection has been with us from the beginning of life, and how its source is spiritual, although it does affect us physically, mentally and emotionally.

We need to consider how Jesus identified with rejection from the beginning of his life in the womb of Mary through to his death on the cross, and understand that he did so in order to set us free from its grip.

The amazing thing is that Jesus never let rejection overcome or control him. He never manifested any fruit of rejection because the roots were never allowed to take hold. That is fantastic in itself because rejection **did** affect him. Finally along with our sin it helped kill him, and even that was turned to good as he rose from the dead.

His birth and early life

An angel appearing to a young lady, probably 16 years old, is one thing, but having Gabriel himself tell her she is going to have a baby is something else! Luke 1:26-38 sets it out in detail. The problem was that she was pledged to Joseph (Matthew 1:18-20) and under Jewish law it was as serious as marriage. Mary could have been stoned. Can you imagine the emotional problems this caused with the couple, the family and probably the village? Not much remained secret! Joseph struggled so much that he decided to break the contract and not marry her. It was not his baby. So whose was it? Did the Holy Spirit really seed her? It took an angel to convince Joseph, and he finally married her. Imagine the gossip, the scandal, the rumour, and this was just the beginning.

It was the time for a census in the Roman world (Luke 2:1), and the family had to go to the home town of Bethlehem to register. It was at least a 3-day journey, and for a pregnant woman very difficult. There was not much care and when they arrived at Bethlehem there was no room for them. Surely Joseph had family there, and I wonder why they could find no accommodation? Was it just because there was no room? There was nothing except a stable which was more like a cave, and Jesus was born with animals around him.

Can you sense the rejection here? It's not the best start in life. Regretfully that is not all, for the ruthless King Herod, realising through the prophetic Scriptures that the Messiah was to be born, wanted to kill Jesus. It seems that after presenting Jesus in the Temple (Luke 2:22-25), and offering a sacrifice which was the custom (they were so poor they could not afford a lamb, and doves or pigeons had to do), they fled to Egypt. Herod in his fury had all the male children 2 years old and under killed. The family remained in Egypt until Herod died. They then returned to an obscure, very poor town called Nazareth, where Joseph set up his business.

When Jesus was 12 years old, he went with his family to Jerusalem. It was an annual event, but at 12 the young men prepare to take their place in the religious community. A crisis occurred, for Jesus went missing. I am not sure that we can sense the great problems this caused. He was missing 3 whole days! They finally found him in the Temple (Luke 2:43-52). Tempers were frayed, and there was a lot of reaction and misunderstanding. Why would a 12 year old boy spend 3 days in the Temple? The emotional pressure on Jesus must have been great. "Why?" they cried, "don't you care about us?" "Why have you treated us like this?" They didn't understand his reply, that he had been in his Father's House. There was a conflict in relationships, yet Jesus became obedient and went down to Nazareth with them. Did the misunderstanding add to the rejection?

As we summarise the beginnings of Jesus' life we can see the potential effect of rejection through family disapproval.

His period of ministry

Throughout the 3½ years of his ministry, the overriding factor was that Jesus was rejected by virtually everyone. He even talked about it himself in order to prepare the disciples for the crucifixion.

His own people

Rejection started in his home town when, after speaking in the synagogue, the people were so furious that they drove him out of town to throw him over a cliff (Luke 4:28-30). Later they took offence again and put Jesus down very cynically, asking where a simple carpenter could get wisdom and miraculous powers. Their unbelief was great (Matthew 13:53-58).

They called him a Samaritan, which was a great insult to a Jew in those days, and more than once said that he had a demon (John 7:20).

They did not like him going to the house of a 'sinner'. Zacchaeus was happy though, because Jesus met him in his rejection and accepted him (Luke 19:7).

At the end the Jews demanded the death of Jesus and continually mocked and insulted him as he hung on the cross (Matthew 27:39).

This can all be summed up in John 1:10-11, *'he was in the world, and though the world was made through him, the world did not recognise him. He came to that which was his own, but his own did not receive him.'*

The Leaders of the people

It is amazing how they rejected him. From the very beginning there was trouble because everyone saw that Jesus had authority and power (Luke 4:36), and that was rare in those days. Jesus began to affect the common people who followed him gladly. He began to undermine the traditions of Jewish society such as the Sabbath, and the religious and political leaders saw their hold begin to slip. So they began to plot against him.

They claimed he was a blasphemer (Mark 2:6), because he talked about forgiving sins.

They criticised him when he ate with 'sinners' and 'tax collectors' (Mark 2:16).

When he healed on the Sabbath, they plotted to kill him (Mark 3:6).

They announced that Jesus was demonized (Mark 3:22).

The leaders condemned him because some of his disciples ate 'the wrong' food (Mark 7:5).

They were continually pushing Jesus to prove his miraculous power (Mark 8:11).

The leaders tried to catch him out with very awkward questions (Mark 10:2-12).

Jesus' authority was continually questioned by them and not in the best spirit (Mark 11:28).

They tried to catch him out in his words (Mark 12:13).

The chief priests and the whole Sanhedrin finally tried to get evidence against Jesus to condemn him. They couldn't without false accusation (Mark 14:55-59).

The leaders insulted and mocked him as he hung on the cross (Mark 15:31).

His family

Incredibly even his family showed Jesus rejection.

They wanted to take 'charge' of him because they thought he was out of his mind (Mark 3:21).

Basically they did not believe in him (John 7:5).

His disciples, his friends

The amazing thing is that even after 3 years with Jesus,

continuously, not one of his friends was with him at the end.

His message was a hard message even to the extent that many of his disciples turned back and no longer followed him (John 6:66).

He was betrayed by one of the disciples, Judas (Luke 22:3-7, 47-48).

When Jesus said to them that they would fall away they denied it (Matthew 26:35), but we know what happened.

Even Peter, who seemed to take the lead in declaring he would never fall away, even to the extent of saying, *"I am ready to go with you to prison and death,"* denied him at the end (Luke 22:23).

At his greatest trial, before the cross, in the garden of Gethsemane, his friends fell asleep. He came to them 3 times in anguish and found them heavy with sleep each time (Mark 14:37-41).

Everyone deserted him and fled, even a young man that was with him, who was seized by the guards, tore himself away and fled naked (Mark 14:50-52).

His own words

Jesus repeatedly foretold his coming rejection and death.

Luke 9:22 – *'the Son of Man must suffer many things and be rejected by the elders, chief priests and the lawyers.'*

Luke 9:44 – *'the Son of Man is going to be betrayed into the hands of men.'*

Luke 17:25 – *'but first he must suffer many things and be rejected by this generation.'*

Luke 18:32 – *'he will be handed over to the Gentiles. They will mock him, insult him, flog him, spit on him and kill him.'*

Yet his friends were so slow to understand him. After the resurrection they remembered his words (Luke 24:8).

His greatest rejection

Nothing can be more horrific and gruesome than being crucified. Accounts have been written describing physical and mental pain and agony that one suffers. Jesus went further, for the spiritual side had to be dealt with. This meant Jesus taking upon himself at the cross our sin, and also being rejected by his Father.

Isaiah 53 sums it up, *'he was despised and rejected by men, a man of sorrows and familiar with suffering. Like one from whom men hide their faces he was despised, and we esteemed him not. Surely he took up our infirmities, griefs and sicknesses and carried our sorrows and pain, yet we considered him stricken by God, smitten by him and afflicted. He was pierced for our transgressions, he was crushed for our iniquities and the punishment that brought us peace was upon him... the Lord has laid on him the iniquity of us all... yet it was the Lord's will to crush him and cause him to suffer.'*

His greatest rejection was made manifest on the cross when he cried, *"my God, my God why have you forsaken me?"*

The rejection of Jesus was made complete at the cross when the Father turned His back on His son. Why? It was their love for you and me that made it happen. The cross then became a 'divine exchange' for us. Instead of being and feeling rejected, we can receive healing, acceptance, affirmation, love, security and so much more through the death and resurrection of Jesus.

8

Dealing with Rejection

As we begin this chapter we need to see that even though God has dealt with rejection through His Son, there is a responsibility on our side to do something about it. Our response should not be passive; faith is always active and we can move towards possessing areas of rejection in our own lives in the power of Jesus' name. Consider Obadiah 17: *'But on Mount Zion will be deliverance; it will be holy, and the house of Jacob will possess its possessions.'* We need to possess that which has already been given to us in Christ! So in terms of rejection, that must mean acceptance and affirmation. We need to see our responsibility as well as God's in this.

Responsibility

This can be defined as recognising that we have a part to play in healing and wholeness and being prepared to do something about it. We need to answer for our own conduct, behaviour, feelings and actions. Personal accountability for some Christians seems rare. We need to own our responsibility with regard to rejection even though the enemy may have got in or some hereditary link is now affecting us. Our behaviour is our behaviour! As we see this and own it, the process of healing will come easier.

When Jesus began his ministry, he made an incredible pronouncement to his own people. *"The Spirit of the Lord is on me, because he has anointed me to preach good news to the poor. He has sent me to proclaim freedom for the prisoners and recovery of sight to the blind, to release the oppressed, to proclaim the year of the Lord's favour."* He went on to say,

"Today this Scripture is fulfilled in your hearing" (Luke 4:18-21). We know that Jesus took responsibility for that statement and his ministry, life, death and resurrection has brought it to pass. We can see and understand the responsibility of God in all of this and are thankful.

Revelation demands a response; we need to take action.

The Fatherheart of God

In the whole area of dealing with rejection it is essential that there is a recognition and understanding of the Fatherheart of God. Many people with rejection have been affected by their parents. This has an effect in later life in their relationship to God as a Father, for they cannot accept easily His love for them and they find it hard to love Him back. Many Christians find it easy to worship God from a distance. He is on the throne, surrounded by the elders etc. Thunders and lightnings penetrate the heavens and we worship in the fear of the Lord. Yet God has another side to His character. He is a Father.

There is a word that is used only 3 times in the New Testament. It is **'Abba'**. Jesus used this word once in his response to God. He was in the garden of Gethsemane (Mark 14:36), praying to the Father and he called him **'Abba'**. This is the first time anyone ever used that word to address God. It is used very much in Jewish culture when a child addresses daddy, and is also used by adult sons and daughters as a warm, familiar, respectful response to their fathers. It is used as an every day response of trust and obedience, **never** to God! Jesus broke through that and used the word in his response to God. To the Jews it was new and unheard of and it expressed a unique relationship with God.

This word is taken up in Romans 8:15 and Galatians 4:6 and it is released to the Church. So we have the right to express our love to the Father by saying to Him, **'Abba'**. We have been adopted into the family of God and he said to us, *"I will be a Father to you, and you will be my sons and daughters"* (2 Corinthians 6:18).

Not only can we call Him **'Abba'**, in our love to Him, but His love to us is so great. God the Father is seeking to give us security, permanence, peace, emotional stability, affirmation and acceptance. Rejection is a barrier to that. God knows us and loves us. Look at His response to Jesus in Luke 3:21-22. The Father actually shouted out from the heavenlies, *"this is my son whom I love and in whom I am well pleased!"* What a response from God! I believe He was so excited that He couldn't help releasing His love for His son. I now know that He loves us exactly the same!

Our identity is found in relationship, firstly accepting God as Father, then understanding that He accepts us, and finally that we can accept ourselves and others.

Isaiah 41:9-10 underlines this, *'you are my servant; I have chosen you and not rejected you. So do not fear, for I am with you.'*

Planning Prayer for Healing

Finally this stage is reached. However, before prayer it is important to consider some issues that should make the prayer for healing/deliverance less difficult.

There should be clarity with regard to understanding the areas that need prayer, i.e. what roots or fruit to be prayed into.

Then we need an understanding with regard to the ways in which we pray, i.e. how to confront any demonic power oppressing the person, or how to release the Holy Spirit in hurt emotions or memories.

There may well be a need to prepare for the time of ministry by fasting or reading specific Scriptures.

Then it is important to recognise our own responsibility to change. The following must be acknowledged:

Disappointment

This can hinder any response to healing. Many rejected people live in the proverb *'hope deferred makes the heart sick'* (Proverbs 13:12). There has been a failure to fulfil the deep and longing expectation for affection and acceptance and a wound of rejection has entered. Out of this frustration and hurt the enemy will look for a foothold as relationships suffer.

Shame

The reaction to being rejected often leaves a sense of humiliation or shame in a person. This can easily open the door for self-rejection and self protection because the enemy will seek to take advantage of the negative situation by the whispers of accusation and condemnation. Because of the fear of more hurt, it is easier to suppress feelings and withdraw. However painful past events are, it is important to face these areas with the grace of God because they can become strongholds in their own right.

Repentance

It is important that repentance is clearly understood. It is more than a quick prayer. We often make it too cheap. Repentance is a costly issue! It is a change of heart, will, thinking and emotions. It is a deliberate turning away from the sin and a clear turning into God with a change of lifestyle.

1. Is repentance necessary with rejection? Yes…! Rejection is SIN! Rejection leads us to sin against ourselves, others and the one who created us. Often our wrong reactions to other people, which come out of our rejection, are not necessarily seen as sin. We need to think again.

2. Look at the way David repented in Psalm 51. David responded clearly and cleanly to the Word of God. He could have been tormented by unforgiveness but when **he** saw that he was the problem, he took responsibility and responded to God and God met him.

3. 2 Corinthians 7:8-10 is a key; *'godly sorrow'* brings

repentance, *'worldly sorrow'* brings death. There is pain in repentance, maybe we need to expose this a little more. This takes time and we should not be afraid of that.

4. Acts 2:37 indicates an important area in repentance, *'when the people heard this, they were cut to the heart, and said to Peter and the other Apostles, "Brothers, what shall we do?"'* We know that Peter said, **"Repent!"** The people had been affected by God's Word which had penetrated into their hearts and they responded accordingly. We need to be open to God's Word in the same way. It is then that repentance becomes effective.

Unforgiveness

It is vital to look at forgiveness and unforgiveness in the context of rejection. There will be someone to forgive who has hurt you, or someone that you hold unforgiveness against. This could include yourself or God.

There is a key story in Matthew 18:21-35.

It shows up the issue of unforgiveness in a very clear light. The servant who was forgiven so much could not forgive at all!

Someone has said, "he that cannot forgive others breaks the bridge over which he must pass himself, for every man has need to be forgiven."

"Everyone says forgiveness is a lovely idea, until they have someone to forgive", says C.S. Lewis.

How does this affect us?

1. We have been forgiven much. It far exceeds any amount that we might have to forgive. We have been forgiven a debt that we could never pay and is far, far in excess of anything that we would ever have to forgive.

2. Here the master's grace and mercy is motivated by

forgiveness, and his anger motivated by the unforgiveness of the servant. How does that apply to God and us with regard to any unforgiveness we might have?

3. Unforgiveness is sin, no matter what has happened to you. The issue is not who is right or wrong, but forgiveness.

4. Unforgiveness will be judged by God.

5. Unforgiveness imprisons the one who cannot forgive. They are held captive.

6. Those in prison or captive will be subject to torture and torment. Unforgiveness can create an entrance for demonic powers.

The conclusion of all this is that unforgiveness can be a great barrier in our relationship to God as well as to each other. When Jesus died, all the barriers went down. Read Ephesians 2:14-16, Colossians 2:13-15. If any barriers are there, they are not on God's side, they can only be with us.

Forgiveness may need to be a process. You may have to keep forgiving until the pain goes. How long is that? Until the pain goes. It certainly is an act of will and we have to decide to forgive before our emotions entangle us. We need to be willing to forgive, not just feel it, and keep on forgiving until the pain goes.

If someone has hurt us, it can:

1. Affect the way we see them. Forgiveness will begin to change our vision.

2. Affect the way we feel about them. Forgiveness will begin to affect the strong feelings we have about them and dissolve them into a neutral place. How can we say we are right with God but not with each other? As we forgive and receive forgiveness, so God will begin to soften us, and who knows the compassion and love that might come in order to bless them or pray for them?

3. Affect the way we talk about them and to them. Forgiveness will change the tongue to a place of more positive talk.

4. Affect our basic attitude and rights. Forgiveness will dissolve the right to get even.

5. Affect our ongoing relationship and hinder any new beginning.

Forgiveness is so important in the area of healing and deliverance. God had no obligation to forgive us, yet He did. We need to get to the place where we can forgive others.

The Healing Process

There are many other books, including some in this series, that already deal with the practicalities of healing and deliverance, therefore I only intend to make a few important comments.

Inner Healing

We need to realise that whatever has been fed into our emotions, memories etc., will not disappear. They remain and can be harmful if of a negative nature, such as rejection. Inner healing will then become necessary. Someone has said that 'inner healing is a ladder, not a single rung; a process, rarely a one-time event'. Therefore counsel and prayer for healing needs to bear this in mind because in the pressure to get things sorted out, it is easy to be insensitive.

Consider Hebrews 13:8, *'Jesus Christ is the same, yesterday, today and forever'*. This is a key scripture with regard to inner healing. Jesus is not affected by our concept of time and space. He is outside it, yet breaks into it in his relationship with us through the Holy Spirit. So if he is the same today as he is yesterday, surely, he can heal yesterday's problems and hurts today.

With inner healing we need to acknowledge the wounds, hurts and memories and surrender them to Jesus, asking the Holy Spirit to bring healing. This may take time and there may be a release of emotion. Let it happen and don't push the feelings of pain down. Give them to Jesus.

Healing from the Demonic

Learn to discern (1 Corinthians 12:10). We need to distinguish what is from God, or from ourselves, or what is demonic, and sometimes it's not easy.

When you are clear there is some demonic intrusion, go to prayer by being specific in taking authority and in casting out the demon (Luke 11:20-22).

Sometimes there is a struggle with a manifestation of some kind. Press through and don't be afraid to have more than one session.

Finally ask the peace of the Holy Spirit to fill the emptiness.

It is quite possible that with rejection, both deliverance and inner healing are necessary. Often in ministry, I have found myself working with both. Be aware of this.

Reconciliation

Finally, broken relationships can be restored. We have been reconciled to God through the cross. We can be restored to each other, sometimes to ourselves and to God in the same way. There has been a change from enmity to friendship. With rejection the above areas lead to restored relationships, as deep wounds and hurts are healed and trust is restored. It is the peace of God that finally rules, and there is no fear. This may take time, so don't rush insensitively into things.

Breaking Bread/Communion

Jesus said, *"do this in remembrance of me."* As we come away from our rejection, breaking bread or Holy Communion can be relevant. We can consider his rejection and our acceptance and affirmation in the light of the cross. Yet he rose from the dead to give us authority by his Spirit to live in freedom so that we can be sure that in our relationship with God there is identity, security and esteem.

9

Moving on from Rejection

Who would have chosen a failure like Peter to preach on the day of Pentecost? So many of us can identify with him in the way he was disloyal to Jesus, which led to the sense of rejection and self-rejection. It's amazing to realise that one moment Peter, with the others who were so supportive of Jesus, were vowing never to leave him, then suddenly he was deserting him with oaths and curses. It's no wonder Peter went outside and wept bitterly (Luke 22:62).

Finally he went back to work, to the old ways, but that was not to be, for Jesus appeared on the lakeside and confronted him. It was out of this that purpose was put back into Peter. Peter denied Jesus three times (Luke 22:34), and Jesus confronted Peter three times (John 21:15-19). Jesus did not let go and finally Peter was restored. Out of this he received identity, direction and revelation about the future. He was healed from the past, restored into the present and given purpose for the future.

The issue of rejection is so great for so many, that it is important to see that pastoral care follows on from prayer for deliverance and healing. It doesn't seem right that after deep ministry, people should be left to carry on in isolation regardless of what they have just been healed from. Some, however, want the prayer but not the discipleship. Sometimes we think the enemy will not bother us again, so therefore we neglect the basic disciplines that we need, to grow away from the rejection and into maturity in our walk with Jesus. Part of the role of the church is to disciple, and in this context the church needs to own its responsibility.

Strategy

Planning ahead is crucial after the time of prayer. It is easy to

67

stand still, but that is like going backwards. Moving on will need wise management and this means good and honest relationships, and being prepared to talk and pray things through. Being alone is not the answer. Planning together is the way forward. So consider what is necessary in your own life to maintain the healing and deliverance received. It is sensible that you plan certain times when you can report on how you are feeling, assessing strengths and weaknesses, and praying together. If you know the care is continuing and that you have good access to it, you will be secure enough to press forward. If the person who prayed with you originally is not able to continue with you in care, make sure that there is someone in your local church who is able to be available. Check this out with your leaders. Do not remain alone hoping things might turn out to be better.

Goals

Once you have thought about an overview, then get down to the specifics. They are disciplines and we need to understand our responsibility in carrying them out. It is important to have something to aim for because discipleship and growth does not just happen!

The following areas need to be considered as goals:

1. *Communication.* Sometimes after prayer for healing and deliverance there is some disorientation in thoughts and emotions, so good and consistent communication is vital. There needs to be responsibility in seeing this through and accountability in being honest with regard to where you are.

2. *Living in the Holy Spirit.* Getting a right understanding of the power of the Cross and the crucified life has to be important in our ongoing warfare with the flesh and demonic powers.

3. *The place of Scripture.* How we read, apply and live out of the reservoir of the Scripture is essential to our freedom in Jesus.

4. ***Prayer and Praise.*** Learning to communicate with God again and thanking Him for what he has done in releasing you, is part of the process of growth.

5. ***Renewing the Mind.*** The battleground is almost always the area of emotion, thought and will. The enemy will continually attack in that area. In Christ we can control the way we think, and use our emotions and our will. We can renew our mind using the disciplines mentioned.

6. ***Learn to Confess Positively.*** Being positive does not mean unreality! The way we talk about ourselves needs to be challenged continually. Look at 1 Corinthians 14:3. It mentions edify – build up, exhort – stir up and comfort – cheer up!

7. ***The Fatherheart of God.*** This is such a key in growth. Learn to relate to God as Father.

8. ***Masculinity/Femininity.*** Many rejected people have problems as to who they really, and how that is worked out. However sensitive that is, our gender and sexuality need to be looked at.

9. ***Esteem/Confidence.*** Often our self-worth and value has been undermined with rejection. It needs reviving and working on. This is important. Do not, however, recognise failure as defeat.

10. ***The Body of Christ.*** Do not isolate yourself from the Church. Get involved in some kind of service, and who knows, you may end up helping others who have been rejected.

11. ***Submit and Resist.*** Many of us resist the enemy but fail to submit to God (James 4:7). The enemy is no respecter of persons, yet we need to understand the authority we have in Jesus, and how to use it. Submit to God first!

12. ***Expectations.*** We get what we expect, so expect freedom. Don't dwell in the past, look forward with reality.

13. ***Laughter.*** Someone has said that humour minimises the intensity of both fear and anger. There is not enough laughter and joy in the church let alone the world! The joy of the Lord is our strength (Nehemiah 8:10). Sometimes we seem afraid of this. Yet God has a sense of humour. Let's enjoy all of His character!

In summary, be responsible for your actions and words, and as you trust the Holy Spirit to guide you, and others to support you, you will grow and mature in your walk in Jesus. Learn to live in the opposite spirit to rejection. Remember failure is not defeat. We do make mistakes, we are human but in Christ we can learn to overcome.

10

Appendix:
Questions Regarding Family History

In the counselling procedure, I have found it very helpful to ask a series of questions relating to the history of the counsellee. Not only does it save time by using this method but it can also pinpoint specific issues which can then be followed up. I have often given the questions at the beginning of the counselling time and asked the counsellee to get back to me after a week or two, which gives them time to answer them honestly and clearly.

These questions will open up a person regarding issues in their life and family that could be important to their healing. Asking the right question is of course vital, and as they are looked at we need to trust the Holy Spirit to bring up the right ones when we are counselling. They are not in any order and the object will be to get the person to open up as much as possible from conception to birth, and right through to where they are today.

1. What is your first memory?

2. Were you wanted?

3. Was there an attempted abortion?

4. Was there a miscarriage before your birth?

5. Did they want a boy and you were a girl? (and vice versa)

6. Was the birth traumatic?

7. Was there bonding to mother?

8. Did she reject you?

9. Who brought you up?

10. How well did you know your father?

11. Was he away much?

12. Was there affection, touch and kiss from your father or mother or both?

13. What is your unhappiest memory?

14. Who was the dominant force in your home?

15. What are the earliest memories you have of your parents?

16. Were there problems or traumas between parents?

17. How did they relate?

18. Whose lap would you sit on?

19. Were there favourites in your family?

20. Did you relate well to your brothers/sisters?

21. Were you illegitimate?

22. What was your order of birth?

23. How were you disciplined?

24. Who disciplined you?

25. Did your parents listen to you?

26. Was anyone always right in your family?

27. Could they be bothered with you?

28. Can you remember any of your parents turning away when you wanted help?

29. Were you favoured in any way in your family?

30. Were any members of your family favoured over and above you?

31. Did you try and get attention from your parents? Both? By what means?

32. Was your father dominant, austere, severe, legalistic with you?

33. Did your parents put religious pressure on you?

34. Can you remember any negative word that anyone of your family put into you?

35. Are your parents together? Happy?

36. If not, are they separated or divorced?

37. What happened to you regarding the above?

38. Did you like school? What about memories?

39. Did you go to a boarding school? At what age?

40. Do you like yourself?

41. Do you dislike or feel threatened by men/women?

42. Are you a regular eater?

43. Are there times when you eat more or less?

44. Are there unusual eating habits in your family?

45. Have you ever thought about an overdose or suicide?

46. Do you dream? If so, what sort? Consistent?

47. Are you or have you been tormented at night?

48. Do you have sexual pressures/thoughts?

49. Where/how did you learn about sex?

50. Have you engaged in extra-marital sexual activities?

51. Do you feel angry with people?

52. Were you sexually abused or tampered with?

53. Were you abused physically or mentally?

54. Do you have strange feelings towards persons of the same sex?

55. Do you feel ashamed?

56. Have you any feeling of guilt?

57. Have you been used for lust (money, sex, power) rather than loved for yourself?

58. Is there anyone you have difficulty in forgiving?

59. Have you experienced great failure or disappointment, been let down or betrayed?

60. How do you relate to authority figures?

61. Were you dominated by anyone in your family?

62. Have you any habits you can't control?

63. Are you afraid of anything or anyone?

64. Have you felt dominated by your husband/wife?

65. Have you been in a failed marriage?

66. Do you feel the victim of the failure?

67. Do you feel discarded because of your failed marriage?

68. Have you been used or abused in your marriage?

69. Are you a single parent?

70. Do you feel hurt, misunderstood and rejected as one?

71. Do you feel discarded by the church?

72. Do you have a problem towards leadership in the church regarding the above?

73. Do you find it difficult to make relationships in the church?

74. Do you have any family in the church? Do you find difficulty in that? Is there any pressure you feel from them?

75. Have you been unemployed?

76. Have you been rejected for a job?

77. Is there any Freemasonry in your family?

78. Is there superstition in your family?

79. Are you aware of any family involvement in spiritism, seances, magic, faith healing, tarot cards or ouija board?

80. Have you been hypnotised?

81. Have you been involved in any of the martial arts, yoga or transcendental meditation?

82. Have you felt you have let down God and His church?

83. Have you felt rejected by God because you have failed Him?

84. Do you long for affection and love?

85. Are you an emotional person?

86. Is it internal or external?

87. Do you find it hard to express your emotions?

88. What happens to them?

89. Are they suppressed and do they come out in an explosion or do they hurt you inside?

90. Do you weep very much?

91. Are there particular reasons why?

92. Do you feel things deeply within but can't get them out for fear of being too emotional, or when attempting to speak, choke them out?

93. Are you afraid if you affirm your own children they will become proud?

94. If you affirm them are you tempted to have a dig as well?

95. Are you afraid if you affirm people too close to you, they will take advantage of you?

96. Do you love your family with actions or words?

97. Do you know God's affirmation or do you hear 'do more'?

98. Do you say good things to other people?

99. When in conversation, do you think of how to respond or do you listen?

100. Do you say what people want to hear in order to please them?

101. Do you want to justify what you do? Why?

102. Do you have difficulty in taking people at face value?

103. Do you always have to defend yourself from attack even with positive criticism?

104. Do you find it difficult to apologise, even to friends? Do you think they may overlook things?

105. Do you think that if you admitted your failings people may reject or abandon you?

106. Has God ever said to you, "you're forgiven"?

107. Is God your 'Abba' (Romans 8:15)?

If you have enjoyed this book and would like to help us to send a copy of it and many other titles to needy pastors in the **Third World**, please write for further information or send your gift to:

Sovereign World Trust, P.O. Box 777, Tonbridge, Kent TN11 9XT, United Kingdom

or to the **'Sovereign World'** distributor in your country. If sending money from outside the United Kingdom, please send an International Money Order or Foreign Bank Draft in STERLING, drawn on a **UK** bank to **Sovereign World Trust**.